The Cradle and the Star

An Advent Study for Adults

Reginald Mallett

Abingdon Press
NASHVILLE

THE CRADLE AND THE STAR:
AN ADVENT STUDY FOR ADULTS

Copyright © 1996 by Abingdon Press

This book is printed on recycled, acid-free paper.

Library of Congress Cataloging-in-Publication Data

Mallett, Reginald.
    The cradle and the star : an Advent study for adults / Reginald Mallett.
      p. cm.
    ISBN 0-687-02128-6 (pbk. : alk. paper)
      1. Advent—Meditations.   2. Advent—Study and teaching.
I. Title.
BV40. .M34   1996
242'.33—dc20   96-22535
                                                                          CIP

Scripture quotations are from the New Revised Standard Version Bible, copyright © 1989, by the Division of Christian Education of the National Council of the Churches of Christ in the United States of America.

Those noted KJV are from the King James Version of the Bible.

96 97 98 99 00 01 02 03 04 05—10 9 8 7 6 5 4 3 2 1

MANUFACTURED IN THE UNITED STATES OF AMERICA

To my grandchildren
Daniel, David, Esther, Joshua, and Martin
with love

Contents

Introduction

The Cradle

"What can we use for a crib?" It was the midwife who asked the question. She had summoned me to a poor home in a remote area hoping that I could succeed where she had failed. She had tried to persuade a young woman who was in early labor to go to the hospital. I also failed. The expectant mother was adamant in her refusal. She had vowed that her first baby would be born at home and our united entreaties could not shake her resolve.

It was mid-December, and events had taken the couple by surprise. The baby was arriving three weeks early. As a newly qualified doctor, I was profoundly grateful for the presence of such a wise and experienced midwife. Thankfully, the delivery went well. Then, as the mother held her newborn daughter, we realized that no provision had been made for a cradle. The midwife, a very practical woman, went to her car and returned with a strong cardboard carton. With some minor modifications and suitably lined, it sufficed.

As I left two happy and thankful parents and drove home through streets lined with shops made bright with festive Christmas lights, I thought of the child in her improvised cradle. It was not the first time that a humble object had been adapted for such a noble use. Once a manger, an animal feeding trough, served a similar purpose. A manger, just pieces of wood no doubt crudely joined together, became the cradle for the Savior of the world. Hymn-writer Charles Wesley captures the wonder of it in his lines:

> Stand amazed ye heavens at this!
> See the Lord of earth and skies;
> Humbled to the dust he is
> And in a manger lies.

At Bethlehem we see the humanity of God in coming as a helpless baby and relying upon an earthly mother for warmth and food. As we begin our Advent journey and look forward to the hope of the ages being fulfilled in Christ, we are reminded that when God stepped onto the stage of recorded history, very ordinary instruments were used. God chose a poor young couple, a rustic animal shelter, and an improvised cradle. The manger has become a symbol of the God who fully shares our helplessness and humanity.

But also a Star!

The star is the symbol of the other part of the Advent story. It reminds us that Christmas is not just about a simple devout couple and a baby, but also about God and a love which reaches out to humanity. Two great theological words grasp hands in this holy season. The first is *immanence*— God here with us, represented by the manger, a humble cradle. The second is *transcendence*—God beyond us, altogether other, eternal, and all-powerful, represented by the star.

With the arrival of Advent Sunday our spirits begin to rise. Cheerful festive decorations appear in the stores and the streets. Sprigs of holly, frosted windows, candles, and colored lights work their Christmas magic. Memories of childhood return. For Christians, however, Advent has much deeper significance. For many whose hearts ache with inexpressible fears and hurts, this wonderful season offers a comfort which cannot be found in any gaily wrapped present, no matter how generous or how kindly meant. Advent offers *hope*. The hope that God is at work in the world. The hope that human sinfulness will not have the final word. The hope that there is a road which stretches from the cradle to the star along which we ordinary folk may travel to the heart of God.

In his book *Principalities and Powers* (Epworth Press, 1952, p. 40), my friend and teacher Professor Gordon Rupp tells of a moving story which emerged during the Nuremberg war crimes trials at the end of World War II. A large number of Jews were being mown down by machine-gun fire across open graves. Among them stood an old man and a little boy. Before they died, the old man bent down and spoke to the boy. What he said will never be known, but as they died the old Jew raised his right arm and pointed to the sky. In the end that is the story of the people of God as from the beginning they have pointed beyond history to the coming righteousness of God. The Christian church has entered into this heritage. It too, like the spires of its churches, points upward, beyond history to the eternal, from the cradle to the star. The Advent hope is that just as God intervened in history in the baby of the manger, so God's purposes will ultimately be fulfilled in spite of human waywardness and sin. Throughout the season the hope rings out that one day heaven will sing: "The kingdoms of this world are become the kingdoms of our Lord, and of his Christ; and he shall reign for ever and ever" (Rev. 11:15 KJV).

So before we plunge into the joyful preparations for Christmas, before we are overwhelmed by the shopping, the writing of cards, the planning of parties and special services in church, let us pause and reflect on this wonder. Let us journey through Advent thrilled by the immanence and the transcendence of God. Thrilled that God holds in one hand the cradle and in the other the star.

The Friend of God

"Abraham believed God, and it was reckoned to him as righteousness," and he was called the friend of God.
(James 2:23)

A woman lay critically ill in the hospital. Her husband, a rough diamond, was a manual worker whom higher education had passed by. He did not find it easy to express himself as I emerged from her hospital room and sat down to talk with him. Gently, I coaxed the conversation along. His three grown children stood by as I tried to describe her condition in nonmedical terms. I concluded by saying that I was sure she had a fighting chance. Tears of hope and relief welled up in his eyes and then almost immediately he became embarrassed by what he thought was a display of weakness; and he apologized for his tears. I hastened to reassure him. "Don't be ashamed of your emotions," I said. "It is natural for a man to feel so deeply about his wife." He then took my hand in his and in a soft voice almost whispered what at first sounded strange. "She is more than that, doctor," he said. "She is my one true friend."

His words echoed in my mind as I wandered down the hospital corridor after leaving him. No poet could have expressed what this man felt more eloquently: "My one true friend." It was an unusual way of expressing a marriage relationship. It spoke of a bonding which, born perhaps in romance, had been tempered by the experiences of delight and disappointment which he and his wife had shared as they reared their growing family on very limited means. Over the years something precious had been forged between them, a deep loving companionship which he movingly described by saying, "She is my one true friend."

Advent is a season of hope. The longings of the ages were to be fulfilled in the coming of the Christ Child. But the story of God's redemption did not begin in Roman occupied Bethlehem. It is important to set the Advent hope in its historical context, for it began centuries earlier in the tents of a man who had set out on a journey of faith. That man, Abraham, is regarded by three of the world's great religions as a founding father. He is inseparably bound up with the story of God's people.

Abraham alone in the Hebrew Scriptures is singled out from the distinguished gallery of great men and women of faith who prepared the way for the coming of the Messiah and is given a special title. Of all the accolades and laurel wreaths, of all the compliments and honors bestowed on anyone who belonged to the community of faith, none was greater than that given to Abraham. His is the unique honor of being called "the friend of God." Others may have been honored by the title "Servant of God," but no other was called "God's friend."

What was so special about this man who before the coming of the Christ Child should be given so lofty a title? Certainly it did not lie in his saintly character. It may come as a surprise to discover that he was vulnerable and frail. Of course, he was a good man, but the Bible makes no attempt to hide the flaws both in his character and in his somewhat dysfunctional family. And yet with all his faults, he played a pivotal part in establishing the nation that would serve as the crucible in which God would prepare the right conditions for the coming of Jesus. This Advent as we think of the hope which was to be embodied in a child lying in a crude cradle, heralded by a song of angels and signaled by a star, it will help us prepare for Christmas to travel back across the centuries and learn the secret of one who was called "the friend of God."

Abraham became God's friend by obeying God's call.

I was recently asked to introduce Dr. Mathan, the Director of the Christian Medical College and Hospital in Vellore,

India, to a lunchtime audience. The meeting was organized by the local branch of "The Friends of Vellore."

It was an unforgettable experience. A distinguished gastroenterologist, Dr. Mathan directs what is the largest medical center on the Indian subcontinent. The work is supported by forty-six denominations in ten countries, and his responsibilities take him around the world. We were overwhelmed by this gracious, gentle man who almost succeeded in hiding his tremendous scholarship and enormous achievements with his self-effacing modesty.

When he began to speak he did not start with himself or his work. Instead he held us enthralled by relating the story of the call of Ida Skudder, the remarkable woman who began the vast enterprise which he now leads.

It was in 1890 that eighteen-year-old Ida was summoned to India by her father, a missionary doctor, because her mother was ill. She left the United States determined that the visit would be brief. It was her firm resolve, just as soon as her mother had recovered, to return to complete her college education and enjoy the free life of a young woman in a land of opportunity. Become a missionary like so many in her remarkable family? Certainly not!

One night, out there in India, however, everything changed.

Sitting at her desk in her parents' little bungalow, she was disturbed three times by distressed husbands who wanted her to come and assist their young wives who were struggling in difficult childbirth. Custom and caste forbade them accepting the help of her medically qualified father. That would be unthinkable. He was a man! Ida was helpless. Without training she would be more a hindrance than a help. Crestfallen she had to turn them away and then passed the night in disturbed heart searching.

Early the next morning she heard the beating of drums in the village and feared the significance of that ominous sound. With a heavy heart she asked the servant to go and make enquiries about the fate of the three women who had been on her mind all night. He returned to tell her that each of them was dead.

Dr. Mathan went on to tell us how that day Ida Skudder was offered a date with destiny. The lives of four young women seemed to reach out and touch one another in the darkness. They never met. They came from different countries. They belonged to different religions; one was a Christian, one a Muslim, and two were Hindus. But the Spirit of God moved over the face of that darkness and planted a hope and a vision in the heart of the eighteen-year-old American girl. In her despair she heard God calling and she kept her date with destiny.

Nine years later, graduating in medicine from Cornell Medical College, Dr. Ida as she became known, returned to Vellore, India, to found a hospital for women and children.

It had not been her original plan to become a missionary. It was not what she had wanted or expected, but she responded in faith. And from that seed of faith a mighty oak has grown. Because she obeyed God a vast enterprise far exceeding anyone's imagination has come into being. Today it is a 1,700-bed medical center, the leading hospital and medical school in India with graduates working all over the world from its 84 training programs in medical, nursing, and paramedical fields.

In obedience and faith a young woman obeyed the divine call and became the friend of God. Like Abraham of old, she went out not really knowing where she was going. As a result the sick are healed, the lame walk, the blind see, and the lepers are cleansed. So identified did this woman become with the people of India that a letter from an American friend which had on the envelope just the words "Dr. Ida - India" was delivered to her doorstep. She became the friend of God and the herald of hope to a subcontinent.

It is not such a great leap of thought from this amazing woman in India to a patriarch living thousands of years earlier. God called Abraham on a journey, which had no clear destination. Common sense would have cautioned him against leaving Ur in Chaldea. But he saw the star, the star of God's guiding hand, and he obeyed. "He set out, not knowing where he was going" (Heb. 11:8) and, as a result, became "the friend of God," giving birth to a hope that one day all would share in that divine friendship.

In Advent we are reminded how centuries later this hope was fulfilled in the coming of the Christ Child. As men and women responded in obedience to the call of Jesus, they heard the words "I do not call you servants any longer. . . . I have called you friends" (John 15:15). Obedience is the doorway through which, this Advent, we may enter into a very special relationship with God.

Abraham became God's friend by looking steadfastly to the eternal.

Some years ago I heard a rather pathetic story of a young couple who had bought an old house just outside an English city. They were desperately short of money, so they tried to cut down the expenses by doing the legal work themselves. At first they were ignorant of the fact that a new highway was planned, which would come straight through their house. When they eventually found out, they thought that by making the old house sufficiently presentable they would be able to persuade the authorities to divert the new road in order to spare their home. They spent more than a year working on it, investing every spare moment of their time and every penny they possessed to renovate the old property. Through their efforts they accomplished wonders. They patched up the cracked walls and covered them with attractive wallpaper. Outdated, dilapidated cupboards were replaced with modern ones. They had a new front door and new window frames fitted. Out went the old shabby kitchen cabinets and in came handsome new ones. They even had an electrician friend come and renew the electrical wiring. The house began to look quite smart and they felt proud of their achievements. The couple were confident they were there to stay.

And then it happened. One day a letter arrived telling them that the date for demolition had been set and giving them a month's notice to vacate the property. They were shattered. They thought of all the time, energy, and expense they had put into that old house. So much of themselves had been invested in a building destined to be bulldozed to the ground. They had lost sight of the fact that they were living under an eviction order.

It is a common folly. We easily forget that we are only temporary tenants of the earthly house God has lent us. Our tenure is very limited, and we are foolish if we overlook the wider dimension of eternity. Abraham made no such mistake. The tents he lived in were a continual reminder that he was only traveling through. He never forgot that he was only a temporary resident. "For he looked forward to the city that has foundations, whose architect and builder is God" (Heb. 11:10).

The message of Advent rings out: Look up! See how the God who found in Abraham a friend reached out through the child of Bethlehem to an estranged humanity. "In Christ God was reconciling the world to himself" (2 Cor. 5:19). The wonder of it: Because of the Savior's coming, ordinary men and women might become the friends of God! But there is more. Advent not only points back in time to the marvelous events which happened two thousand years ago. It also points forward, reminding us of the thrilling hope that one day all things will be gloriously summed up in Christ. Happy, therefore, are they who fix their eyes, not on the things which are destined to pass away, but on the things which last forever. Happy, because they thus become the friends of God.

Abraham became God's friend by holding nothing back from God.

Few stories in the Bible so grip the imagination as that in which Abraham is prepared to offer up Isaac to God. It is impossible to understand the patriarch's relationship with God without examining this story carefully.

Here is a picture in two parts. In the first, Abraham accompanied by his happy, carefree son is painfully making his way to the top of a hill with anguish in his heart. The journey begun two days earlier is now reaching its completion. The elderly father and his young son have left the two servants with the donkey down in the valley, and the two of them climb together. As they did so, turmoil must have been boiling in the heart of the old man. Why had he felt an inner compulsion to do something utterly repulsive to all his natural feelings? Why was he so sure that God wanted him to destroy everything that had been so carefully built up? How could a God of mercy want him to do something so merciless?

But he could not escape it. The conviction had grown and grown until it had become an obsession. He must have tossed in his tent, unable to sleep as he struggled with it. We can imagine him standing beneath the open heavens asking the question "Why?" The insistent prodding would not, however, go away; God seemed to want what was most precious in his life. Nothing was to be held back. And for Abraham, accustomed to a culture of sacrifice, this could mean only one thing.

And so the old man toils up the hill with Isaac, who carries the wood on his back for his father's sacrifice. As they near the brow of the hill, the boy voices his bewilderment. "The fire and the wood are here, but where is the lamb for a burnt offering?" The father looks at him with eyes full of pain and love. "God himself will provide the lamb for a burnt offering, my son" (Gen. 22:7-8). What questions Abraham must have been asking himself at that moment. Is this where the dream ends? Is this God's great joke? Does God give with one hand just to take away with the other? Is this the end of that great pilgrimage of faith which started when he responded to God's call in faith and left the security of Ur in Chaldea to set out for a promised land? And what about that promise God made to him and his wife, Sarah, that their descendants would be as plentiful as the stars in the heaven? A grim jest? The family line wiped out forever on that hill? Here is the first act in the drama, Abraham ascending heartbreak mountain.

The second part of the picture is in complete contrast. Now we can envisage the old man and the boy coming down the mountain. Old man? Why, he strides with the powerful, confident step of one years younger. There is a glint in his eyes. The boy skips by his side, delighting in his father's laughter and song. There on that hilltop a special bond was established between Abraham and God. Reverberating in his heart he can hear the word, which he knows came direct from heaven. "Do not lay your hand on the boy or do anything to him; for now I know that you fear God, since you have not withheld your son, your only son, from me"(Gen. 22:12). The words were like a song of redemption. More, they were a song of hope. God was revealed forever as the God of promise. The purposes at the heart of creation would be worked out through the kind of person represented by this towering figure in the story of faith. He held nothing back. He ascended the mountain chained to the past and its practices. He descends the mountain looking to the future with hope shining in his heart.

From that moment on, whenever God came to the early Hebrews, the announcement would be made: "I am the God of Abraham." God Almighty has not just a servant, not just a believer, not just a worshiper, but *a friend*. And here we trace the birth of a hope that this privileged relationship might become the destiny of all who were ready to hold nothing back in their worship and service.

W. E. Sangster tells (*The Pure in Heart*, Epworth Press, 1955, p. 161) of an evangelistic mission which was held in York toward the end of the last century. One night a number of people responded to the invitation, including an elderly man. The evangelist counseled each in turn including this particular man, who meekly answered the questions put to him and then went his way. Later the evangelist learned that the elderly man was saintly David Hill, a most distinguished Methodist missionary in China who happened to be home on leave. He was to return shortly to the country he loved and die of typhus at Hankow.

The preacher sought David Hill out and made a halting apology for having treated him as a beginner in the holy life. David Hill brushed his embarrassments aside. "I thought it would do me good to kneel among the penitents," he said. He had made it his practice never to hold anything back. He was a friend of God.

As we journey through Advent and approach the Savior's cradle, the offering which God most desires is our heart's devotion. When we give that, holding nothing back, we join the select band of those who may be called "the friends of God."

Study Questions

1. Read Genesis 12:1-9 and Hebrews 11:8-10, which record Abraham's obedience to the divine call. Consider some of the ways in which God calls us today. What practical measures will you take this Advent (such as structuring your day to give you more time for daily contemplation and prayer) to make yourself more sensitive to God's call?

2. Read Genesis 22:1-19. What do you think was the significance of this test for Abraham? How would you apply this story to your own spiritual journey?

3. Read Nehemiah 9:6-8, Galatians 3:6-9, John 8:31-40—just three of many examples in the Bible where Abraham is recalled as a model for those who came after. Who are the people who have influenced your Christian journey? What was it about them which affected you most? Are those qualities present in your life? How can they be cultivated?

4. Read Hebrews 11:8-16. Abraham is described as "living in tents," emphasizing the fact that he was "a stranger and a foreigner on the earth." Is the note of heaven and the temporary nature of this life something evidenced in your own discipleship, or do you tend to overlook it? How will you correct this while retaining your social concern for what needs to be corrected in the world about us?

5. Read John 15:12-17. Are there people you find impossible to love? What are the reasons? Is it more difficult to love those who have hurt you or those who have hurt someone dear to you? Consider what positive steps you can take to help you solve this particular problem, such as sharing the difficulty with a pastor or a trusted counselor. What would you say to someone who came to you with this particular problem?

6. Advent is the season of giving. Read Acts 4:32–5:11. What do you think this passage is saying about being honest in what we are willing to give and to withhold from God? What things in your life are you prepared to give and what are those you wish to hold back from God? (Consider relationships in your home, business, church, and community; material possessions; and your use of time.) What positive steps are you willing to take this Advent toward full commitment to God?

Focus for the Week

The birth of the Advent hope can be traced back to Abraham and his relationship with God. "'Abraham believed God, and it was reckoned to him as righteousness,' and he was called the friend of God" (James 2:23). Is trust in God the foundation of your daily living? Are you sensitive to God's call? Do you walk with your eyes fixed on the eternal? Are you prepared to offer to God what is most precious in your life if that be the divine will? Are you the friend of God?

The Touch of God

You shall no longer be called Jacob, but Israel, for you have striven with God and with humans, and have prevailed. (Genesis 32:28)

In our living room we have a corner cabinet with glass doors. It houses pieces of crystal given to us over the years. This modest collection includes things we treasure. In the center of the display there is something a visitor might consider out of place. It is a rather quaint, comic-looking china dog. I think it is supposed to be a poodle. It sits on its haunches with its front paws off the ground. Its cheeks are colored pale pink so that it appears to be blushing. It wears a funny-looking bonnet, which serves as a pin cushion. There is a slot on the bridge of its nose, which holds a small pair of scissors so that it appears to be wearing glasses. Its tail is a spring-loaded eighteen-inch tape measure.

Once when our house was broken into, the intruders took a number of objects they thought were worth something. They ignored the dog, which I can well understand. To them or anyone else, it has no value. To my wife and me, however, it is priceless. Whenever my medical career took us to another part of the country, we did not entrust that little dog to the tender care of the moving men. We did not mind their handling the rest of the glassware and china, but that strange creation was far too precious to be handled by any strangers. Instead it traveled with us, carefully protected from damage. Why does it merit such special protection? Any parent will understand the answer. When she was seven years of age, our daughter emptied her little piggy bank and, without any prompting from her parents, went to the local general store around the corner and bought it for our wedding anniversary. Something very ordinary was made extraordinary when touched by the grace and generosity of a little girl.

Some years ago, in the early hours of a January morning, I was called to the local hospital to baptize triplets who had been born prematurely. Their father, a distinguished scholarly man, aware that their hold on life was precarious, was most anxious that they should receive Christian baptism without delay. He stood beside his wife's wheelchair in the special care unit as I took some water and, reaching inside the incubators, made a cross on each of their tiny heads and said the words of the sacrament. What was so special about that water? To those of us there it had become more than water. The ordinary had become extraordinary because in faith we saw it touched by the grace and generosity of God and made a symbol and sign of Christian hope. Shortly afterward, as had been feared, the most frail one of those three tiny babies died. Once again I stood with the parents—this time in the hospital chapel—and reaffirmed that same hope in the glorious words, "We know that if our earthly house of this tabernacle were dissolved, we have a building of God, [a] house not made with hands, eternal in the heavens" (2 Cor. 5:1 KJV).

The story of the faith is punctuated by ordinary individuals who became extraordinary because they were touched by God's grace and generosity and made symbols of hope. When first introduced to us, some of them do not appear very promising, but as God begins the work of remolding and as they respond to the divine touch we see them becoming different people. Such a one was Jacob. As we see how he responded to God's touch, we can, perhaps, see also what God is doing to us as we make our Advent pilgrimage to Bethlehem. Jacob's story, like ours, may be regarded as a drama in three acts.

Act 1: God—a stranger with whom to strike a bargain.

When we first meet him, Jacob is a shrewd, scheming individual motivated by self-interest. He does not hesitate to take advantage of his brother or deceive his aging father. Thus it is that early in his story he has to flee from home, a fugitive escaping from the anger of Esau whom he has tricked out of his rightful inheritance.

One night, as he travels to the safety of his grandfather's home, he rests at a place he later called Bethel. There he has a strange dream in which he sees a ladder stretching from earth to heaven. A less spiritually sensitive person might have dismissed it as a figment of imagination, but Jacob believes that he has encountered God; and his first words the next morning impress us: "Surely the LORD is in this place—and I did not know it! . . . How awesome is this place! This is none other than the house of God, and this is the gate of heaven" (Gen. 28:16-17). But this good impression is soon shattered as the deceiver tries to strike a bargain with God. "If God will be with me . . . and will give me bread to eat and clothing to wear . . . *then* the LORD shall be my God" (Gen. 28:20, emphasis added). At this stage in his life, Jacob's allegiance and worship are conditional.

A. J. Cronin, in *The Keys of the Kingdom* (Victor Gollancz, 1942), describes how Francis Chisholm, a sincere, dedicated Catholic priest, was sent to China. On his arrival he found that the thriving mission he had been promised was nonexistent. Using his elementary medical knowledge he opened a dispensary. This, at least, met with some response as poor sick people came for help. One day he was dumbfounded when asked to go to see the six-year-old son of Mr. Chia, one of the wealthiest and most influential men of the region. He found the boy dying of septicemia from a grossly infected arm and hand. Risking the appalling consequences should he fail, Chisholm incised the infected limb and drained the life-threatening poison away. Almost immediately the boy started to mend. By his prompt action, Chisholm had saved his life. Next day he returned to check on his patient's progress. As he was leaving, the priest was told that he did not need to come again. Firmly and politely he was dismissed from the case.

For days the priest struggled to quell his anger and indignation at such outrageous ingratitude. And then a week later, just as he was closing the dispensary, he was aware that Mr. Chia, the boy's father, was standing there. It was evidently a formal visit. Chia, dressed in his finest clothes, explained that he had not been able to come earlier because there was much to do. Now, at last, these other details had been dealt with and he had come. "Why?" asked Chisholm. "Naturally . . . to become a Christian" was the answer. Chia then went on to explain that although he did not believe, by becoming a Christian he would in some measure be repaying the debt he owed for his son's life. He was offering himself as his part of the bargain with Chisholm's God.

At that moment everything the priest longed for could have been his. Had Chia become a Christian, the rest of the town would have followed and all Chisholm's problems would be over. There would be no shortage of financial support. Any opposition to the faith would be silenced by the rich man's servants. It was a prospect a lesser person would have eagerly seized. The priest, however, would have none of it. He rejected the offer; the God he served was not in the bargaining business. This was strange to Chia, who thought it natural to settle accounts and keep his end of a contract. He left the dispensary with his offer rejected but with a profound respect for this man of shining integrity, a respect which eventually led to a genuine conversion.

This is where Jacob is on his spiritual journey when he reaches Bethel. As we search our hearts on our Advent journey to Bethlehem, we begin to realize that Jacob is not alone in trying to strike a bargain with God. Often our discipleship is conditional. Yes, we will go on believing, just as long as God keeps us and our loved ones in good health, guards our children from danger, enables our business to prosper, makes us popular with our friends, and provides us with the right partner. This Advent, God is prompting us to move on from this inadequate understanding to something more mature. We are urged to move on beyond Bethel.

Act 2: God—an adversary with whom it is necessary to struggle.

There is a Christian legend that in the town of Jericho, years after the death and resurrection of Jesus, the aged Zacchaeus used to slip out of his villa each morning and evening. According to the story he could be seen going to an outbuilding attached to the villa and emerging with a large earthenware jar. He would fill the jar with water from the well and then, with it on his shoulder, would make his way to the Jerusalem road. There he would lovingly pour the water around the roots of an old sycamore tree, and it was said that there was often the glimmer of tears on his cheeks. Once, when he was crouching beside the tree, someone who did not know his story saw the tears and asked him if he were feeling ill. The old man looked up at his questioner with a seraphic smile and replied, "I am quite well, thank you. But you see, it was here that I met Jesus."

Many people have special times and places when they have been aware of the presence of God. For some it was quite unexpected; for others it came gradually in response to their search for a deeper dimension in their lives. Whether sudden or gradual, it was for them all a transforming encounter. After it happened, nothing could be the same again.

Jacob had such an experience. Years had passed since his treacherous deception of his brother. He had married and prospered. Now, returning to his home country with all his family, his flocks and herds, he heard the worrying news that Esau was coming to meet him with a large number of men. He mistakenly feared that his brother still remembered how he had been deceived and was on his way to settle old scores.

That night, after his entire company had crossed a stream called Jabbok, Jacob had a strange experience which defied description and which has intrigued Bible students ever since. It seemed to him as though he was struggling with a man, but he then discovered that his adversary was in fact God. Although shrouded in mystery it is clear that this was a transforming encounter. After it was over and his struggle with God the adversary was ended, Jacob was a different person. In awe he said, "I have seen God face to face, and yet my life is preserved" (Gen. 32:30).

A young man once came to Jesus. He had reached his Jabbok. "What must I do to inherit eternal life?" he asked. Jesus offered the way: "Sell what you own, and give the money to the poor . . . then come, follow me" (Mark 10:17-21). Here was a struggle in which Jesus was wrestling for this young man's soul and might have been seen as an adversary. In the end the will of the young man triumphed, but it was a hollow victory. He went away sorrowful and missed the greatest opportunity of his life.

There is a stage in our Advent journey when God appears as an adversary challenging all that is unworthy and base in our lives. If we can but see it, we have reached Jabbok. We struggle with our unseen adversary who challenges our selfishness, greed, pride, love of power, and vanity. To surrender and allow God to make us new by touching us with generosity and grace is to be prepared for an experience of the Christ Child. Without this, the celebration of the Savior's birth, instead of being a meaningful spiritual encounter, will be hollow, degenerating into yet another giddy whirl of spending and feasting. When God the adversary triumphs in this struggle for our souls, we become aware, with an overwhelming sense of wonder, that we are considered worth struggling for. Our journey through Advent to the cradle of the Christ Child prepares us for a transforming encounter when we kneel at the manger. Then with joy we will say what Zacchaeus said of the old tree: "It was here that I met Jesus."

Act 3: God—a friend who journeys with us.

Ian Macpherson (*God's Middleman*, Epworth Press, 1965, p. 74) relates how the poet Francis Thompson told of an English lady whom a friend of his happened to meet in Paris. He was about to address her by name in company when the lady put up her hand restrainingly. "Hush!" she whispered. "Don't recognize me! I'm traveling in *embryo!*" Of course she had got the word wrong. She had intended to say "incognito." But without realizing it she was expressing a profound truth. We are all traveling through life in embryo. If we allow God to touch us with the grace and generosity displayed in the coming of the child of Bethlehem, we begin to develop into what the divine plan intended us to be.

For Jacob, the night has ended and his struggle with God is over. As dawn breaks there is still the stream to cross and the threat represented by Esau and his men to face. The future remains uncertain with all its shadows and hurts. But there is now a tremendous difference. His spiritual embryo has undergone a momentous development. God has been experienced as a friend and with that assurance he travels with hope. This transforming encounter displays the wonder of faith, which looks beyond earth to heaven, beyond human weakness and despair to divine power and hope, beyond a cradle to a star. Jacob the trickster who tried to bargain with God has been touched by divine grace and generosity and is so changed that his old name Jacob, "the supplanter," is no longer appropriate. He is to be known as Israel, "the one who strives with God." The essential thing is not what Jacob *was* but what he *became* when touched by God; the ordinary made extra-ordinary.

The heart of the Advent hope is that the God who transformed Jacob came in Jesus to transform the world, and one day that transformation will be complete.

At the church a friend of mine was serving in the north of England, the choir always produced Handel's *Messiah* during Advent. In his final year there, the musical director told him that the soprano soloist he had engaged was blind. My friend's immediate thoughts were of the practical details that would need attention. He arranged for someone to help her up the steps to the platform since she would be in unfamiliar surroundings. The tenor soloist who would be sitting next to her was asked to make sure that she knew where to stand when she sang. The chair selected for her had arms so that she could feel for them as she sat down. Everything had been meticulously planned. My friend said that his mind was not on the performance but on the possibility of some small problem arising.

Then, on the night of the performance during its progress, he found himself suddenly lifted to the heavens. It happened at the point where the soprano and the contralto soloists have to rise together. The choir had just proclaimed in music the glorious fulfillment of prophecy that a child had been born who would be called the prince of peace. The blind soprano then sang in ringing tones, "Rejoice, rejoice greatly O daughter of Zion." As though to expound this message, the contralto gently sang, "Then shall the eyes of the blind be opened and the tongue of the dumb sing. . . . He shall feed his flock like a shepherd," to which the blind soprano responded, "Come unto him all ye that labor and he will give you rest."

Here was the testimony of one who had a right to speak. Because of her blindness, she might have been denied a thousand things others take for granted, but she could rejoice greatly. One day the eyes of the blind *would* be opened. One day the tongue of the dumb *would* sing. One day the God who changed a man such as Jacob *would* complete the work and change the world. This is the glorious Advent hope. But God begins by touching and changing us.

Study Questions

1. Read Genesis 28:10-22, noting especially verses 20-21. Compare these with Daniel 3:16-18. What do you consider to be the main difference between the faith demonstrated in these two passages?

2. "Our family had always lived decent lives. We had attended church regularly and been generous in our support. We had regular times of prayer at home. Why then should God have allowed our son to be killed in a climbing accident?" What does this heartfelt cry reveal about the person's faith? What would you say if these words were addressed to you?

3. Read Genesis 32:22-32, Mark 10:17-22, Mark 14:32-36. Make a list of the things you feel could be in conflict with the will of God in your life, in the church, and in the community. What steps do you intend to take to resolve this conflict on your Advent journey?

4. Read Ephesians 6:10-20. What do you think Paul had in mind

in verse 12? What are the main "spiritual forces of evil" that challenge you and your family today? How can you prepare yourself to meet them?

5. What are the spiritual landmarks in your life? Are there times or places when God has been particularly real to you? What have you learned from such experiences and how have they enriched your journey of faith? Have you shared them with others?

Focus for the Week

Are you still at the bargaining stage in your walk with God? Is your discipleship conditional on things going right for you? Are you still at Bethel? Or have you moved on and found that God is struggling with you, challenging areas of your life to which you still cling? Are you at Jabbok? Or have you crossed over, surrendered to God, and discovered the joy and hope of divine friendship? Are you ready in mind and spirit to make your pilgrimage to the manger and worship the Christ Child?

David's Line

For your daughter-in-law who loves you, who is more to you than seven sons, has borne him. (Ruth 4:15)

It is already the third Sunday of Advent. "Rejoicing Sunday" is the name the church has given to this particular day as Christmas draws near and minds turn to remember with gladness the Savior's first coming in Bethlehem long ago. Christians also rejoice because of the Advent hope that one day there will be a glorious Messianic return in majesty and power.

For many, however, the rejoicing is swamped by a rising tide of panic. How can everything possibly be done in time for the festival? The tree isn't up yet. There are still so many presents to buy. The cards have not been written. There are rehearsals at the church for the nativity pageant. The scattered members of the family will be returning in just over a week and we are nowhere near ready. The days are passing far too quickly. If only time would slow down!

How different when we were children. Then December seemed to last forever. "How many days to Christmas?" I asked several times each day. Patiently my mother would take me to the calendar hanging on the wall and show me how each day was crossed off at its close. "When we come to 24 you will know it is Christmas Eve and time to hang up your stocking," she would say.

To ease our ache of waiting for Christmas, during the evenings of Advent my mother would gather us around her knee by the fire and tell stories. Our favorites were her memories of Christmas spent with her grandparents when she was young. Her eyes sparkled as she recalled how her grandparents, though poor in material things, were wonderfully rich toward God. Little did she realize that in describing to my sensitive mind my two devout forebears she was painting word pictures which would adorn the gallery of my memory all my life. Each Advent I walk through that gallery and as I think of my great-grandparents, I am reminded of my rich heritage of faith.

I wonder if that happened to young David? He was the boy destined to become Israel's greatest king. His reign would be recalled by later ages as being a foretaste of the great Messianic age. When Zechariah, the father of John the Baptist, was expressing his thanksgiving to God he said, "Blessed be the Lord God of Israel, / for he has looked favorably on his people and redeemed them. / He has raised up a mighty savior for us / *in the house of his servant David*" (Luke 1:68-69, emphasis added). God's great deliverer was promised to be "of David's line," and the name of this outstanding king is featured in many of our Advent hymns. What pictures did David's father, Jesse, hang in the gallery of the child's sensitive mind? I feel sure that in the light of the flickering fire Jesse would have recalled David's great-grandmother, a remarkable woman who across the ages has been honored as one of the great figures in the story of faith. Few of us have not been moved by the lovely story of Ruth, who came from the land of Moab.

On the third Sunday of Advent, we rejoice in the knowledge that in the little town of Bethlehem God was about to fulfill the promise of bringing us a deliverer from evil. As we have been reminded already, however, this promise did not begin in Roman occupied Judea when Herod was king. We have seen how, long before the star guided wise men to the cradle, God was carefully laying the foundation of the Advent hope in the tents of Abraham and Jacob. In those same fields around Bethlehem where one day shepherds would hear the angelic announcement of the Savior's birth, young David played and Ruth his great-grandmother followed the reapers, gleaning corn.

It is fitting that on our journey to the cradle of the one who was to be born of David's line, the spotlight should shine for a brief time upon Ruth, this remarkable woman who came from a foreign land. Advent is the time when we anticipate the fulfillment of all the prophetic promises and the final victory of suffering love. Living each day as though it could be the day when Christ will come and bring in that Messianic age is what makes Advent people. If we would join their number, then Ruth can be our guide.

Advent people can be identified by the quality of their living.

Ruth reminds us that to be an "Advent person" involves much more than merely *saying* the right things. Actions speak louder than words. Expensive gifts at Christmas cannot make up for the pain caused to others by being harsh, unkind, and thoughtless. If we are to live in the spirit of Advent, then, not for a brief season only but throughout the year, our lives must have about them a quality which indicates that we are ready for the coming of Christ.

Once when he was preaching in the Cambridge University church, Billy Graham began by recalling a newspaper reporter's question. He had been asked whether or not he thought his sermons had accomplished anything. He disarmed his questioner by humorously relating an incident that had happened to him while on a flight to North Carolina (*Sermons from Great St. Mary's*, ed. High Montefiore, Collins, Fontana Books, 1968). On the plane was a man who was intoxicated. The man's language and conduct were very undesirable. Eventually it was necessary for the flight attendant to call for the assistance of the copilot in order to persuade him to resume his seat. Graham said, "Someone whispered to the drunken man that I was sitting behind him. He got himself up again, turned around and said to me, 'Are you Billy Graham?' I said 'Yes.' Then he said, 'I want to shake hands with you because your sermons have sure helped me.'"

The great evangelist then went on to describe, in contrast, how the church was built not upon empty professions such as that of the man on the plane but upon lives which had been transformed by the impact of the spirit of God. Not just words, but deeds mark men and women as Advent people.

Few passages in all literature can match the words Ruth addressed to her mother-in-law when Naomi decided to return to her home in Judea. Years before, during a time of famine, Naomi with her husband and two sons had left their home and had sought refuge in the foreign land of Moab. After the death of Naomi's husband, her sons fell in love and married local women. A bond of deep affection was forged between the widowed mother and her two daughters-in-law. Then, after the loss of her husband, calamity struck Naomi again. One after the other, her two sons died. Overwhelmed by grief she decided to return to her old home in Bethlehem. When she announced this intention, her two daughters-in-law insisted on going with her. Naomi felt sure that they would have a better chance to rebuild their lives in their own country of Moab and begged them to return to the homes of their parents. One reluctantly followed her advice. Ruth, however, was immovable and in immortal words, exquisitely expressed by the old King James Version, said:

> Entreat me not to leave thee, or to return from following after thee: for whither thou goest, I will go; and where thou lodgest, I will lodge: thy people shall be my people, and thy God my God: Where thou diest, will I die, and there will I be buried: the LORD do so to me, and more also, if aught but death part thee and me.
>
> (Ruth 1:16-17 KJV)

These were noble sentiments. For Ruth, however, they were more than just talk. She robed her words with deeds. Despite the natural reluctance of the people of Bethlehem to accept a foreigner, she stayed by Naomi's side. She did not shrink from lowly work such as gleaning in the fields for corn so that she and her mother-in-law might eat. The story had a happy ending as Ruth married Boaz, a local landowner and kinsman, and, in due time, gave birth to a son. The compliments the local women paid Naomi on having a grandson were all the more powerful because of their earlier suspicions of the stranger from another country. "Your daughter-in-law who loves you, *who is more to you than seven sons*, has borne him" (Ruth 4:15, emphasis added).

David had a worthy great-grandmother. And when Jesus is hailed in our singing as "Great David's greater Son," we call to mind that his descent can be traced back to one who by the quality of her life expressed the meaning of Advent living.

Advent people can be identified by the quality of their loving.

When Ruth accompanied her mother-in-law on that sad journey back to Bethlehem she had no thought for herself. The future was a closed book. In her devotion to Naomi she was not following some hidden agenda of self-interest. Out of love she wanted only to give. There is no mention in her story of any sense of personal loss, still less self-pity or bitterness, even though her husband had been snatched from her when they were both still young. Her own hurts had been swallowed up in self-giving.

Advent is the season when we recall the self-giving of God. Paul quotes an early Christian hymn about Jesus, which says "though he was in the form of God, / [he] did not regard equality with God / as something to be exploited, / but emptied himself, / taking the form of a slave, / being born in human likeness" (Phil. 2:6-7). Jesus taught that they who are prepared to lose their lives in loving service truly find the meaning of life. On this third Sunday of Advent, "rejoicing Sunday," we remember with gratitude how the promised One "of David's line" fulfilled the hope that a reign of love would be established, putting an end to the night of hatred and enmity. Centuries earlier, David's great-grandmother Ruth, by her self-giving love, kept this hope alive during a dark period in the nation's life. In losing herself in service she found herself. And this is the secret of Advent loving.

A formative influence on my life was a Bible class for boys, which I attended each Sunday afternoon. We were a rowdy bunch, and our teacher was a gracious, refined lady whom we knew as Miss Johnson. We thought of her as middle-aged. Looking back I realize that she was probably in her early twenties! In our boisterous and thoughtless behavior, I fear that we must often have taken unfair advantage of her quiet patience.

One Sunday in June 1944 we were particularly noisy. Exciting things were happening. During the preceding week all the trucks and tanks and the tens of thousands of American soldiers, who had been crowded into our town and the surrounding countryside of that part of England, had disappeared as if by magic. Then we heard the news. On June 6, the Allies had launched the massive invasion of Normandy. We were all talking about this at the tops of our voices on that second Sunday afternoon in June when Miss Johnson arrived. She took her seat behind the table, and after an opening prayer she opened her Bible. Her voice was particularly soft and she spoke unusually slowly. We were seated around the table in a semicircle. One of our number had brought a bag of marbles. Miss Johnson had scarcely begun the lesson when he rolled one of them across the floor to the person on the other side of the semicircle and that person rolled it back. We all thought this was hilarious. Soon marbles were rolling in all directions. Miss Johnson then did something she had never done before. She closed her Bible and rose to her feet. In a trembling voice she said, "Boys, you are in no mood for Bible study this afternoon. I am going to say a prayer and then go home." We were instantly subdued. We knew we had gone too far. As she made her way to the door, we could see that Miss Johnson's cheeks were wet with tears.

Next Sunday we gathered at the usual time for the Bible class, feeling quite sure that Miss Johnson would not turn up after our misconduct the week before. We were wrong. She came, on time as usual. The week after that, she came. Similarly, the week after that. Regularly, without a break she continued to lead that class. Miss Johnson never married. Several years later I discovered by chance that her fiancé had been killed on the Normandy beaches during that fateful invasion for the liberation of Europe. She had come to the class on that particular Sunday having just received the news. Her heart was breaking. But instead of allowing self-pity or bitterness to overwhelm her, she lost herself in loving service for the sake of some silly, ill-behaved boys who thought it was clever to roll marbles when she was trying to teach. It is because of such as her that I came to faith. She showed me what Advent loving was all about.

This is a lesson we can all learn from Ruth, the great-grandmother of David. During a dark period in her life, self-giving love shone through the gloom and filled that home in Bethlehem with a radiant light. And, in the fullness of time, the prophetic promises have been fulfilled in one who was born "of David's line." Through Jesus a new race of people has come into being. They live as though each day is the day when the Messianic age will begin. They can be distinguished because of the quality of their loving.

Ian Macpherson tells (*News of the World to Come*, Prophetic Witness Publishing House, 1975, p. 296) of a visitor touring Switzerland who saw on the shore of a beautiful lake a delightful mansion. He was deeply impressed by the large and perfectly kept garden in which it was set. The close-cropped lawns, trim and tidy paths and terraces, and gorgeous flower beds were testimony to loving and unremitting toil on the part of the gardening staff. Not a weed was to be seen anywhere. The tourist paused to admire the scene and, seeing one of the staff, the curator, there in the garden, he praised its order and beauty to him. "How long have you worked here?" he asked. "Twenty years," was the reply. In the conversation which followed, it was disclosed that the owner of the mansion was absent most of the time. "How often has the owner been in residence during your twenty years of service?" the tourist asked. "Four times," replied the curator. The visitor expressed his surprise. "And to think," he exclaimed, "that for all these years you have kept this house and garden in such superb condition! Why, you look after them just as if you expected your master to come tomorrow!" "No," corrected the curator, "I look after things as if I expected my master to come today!"

This is a picture of Advent people. You can tell who they are. They live and love each day as if it were the day of their Savior's coming.

Study Questions

1. Read Ruth 1:15-18: What do you think were the qualities in Naomi which drew this declaration from Ruth? Many families, including those of committed Christians, are under great stresses today. As a result, many suffer fragmentation and dysfunction, with inevitable heartbreak. What can we learn from the relationship between Naomi and Ruth that might help us to meet the stresses presented by our prevailing culture?

2. Many of us find that the pace of life with its many commitments seems to deny us time to walk with one another down the hallway of faith and share stories of how our lives have been influenced by our parents and grandparents. This means that some children are denied part of their inheritance. Suggest ways in which each day may be organized so that there is time for such sharing.

3. Read 2 Samuel 23:15. Do you think that David was longing for the return of his youth? Which moments in your life do you recall with either particular gladness or regret? What lessons have you learned from them? What part does your faith in Christ play in helping you come to terms with your past?

4. Read John 13:1-15. Here is a model of Advent loving that considers no task too menial when performed for others. Do you see opportunities for Advent loving during this Advent season? Is there someone you know who, perhaps, lives alone, is frail or elderly, and for whom you could perform some humble service? Is there some small and inconspicuous task in the church you could undertake? How ready are we to display Advent loving?

5. Ruth, with her self-giving, anticipates Advent and the quality of life to which Jesus introduces disciples. Does our self-giving extend as far as being willing to forgive those who have wronged us? Are you prepared *today* to send them a Christmas greeting together with a brief note expressing your love for them as children of God?

Focus for the Week

Are you an Advent person? Can you be distinguished by the quality of your living and your loving? Are you approaching Bethlehem with a sense of wonder that God can use ordinary people like you, just as Ruth was used so long ago, to keep alive the hope which was fulfilled in the coming of Jesus? Would you be ashamed if Christ were to come in glory today, or would you respond with gladness and thanksgiving?

Mary's Boy Child

And she gave birth to her firstborn son and wrapped him in bands of cloth, and laid him in a manger, because there was no place for them in the inn. (Luke 2:7)

In my youth I heard a preacher tell of an old Englishman who fell on hard times and was compelled to sell his small collection of coins. He asked a dealer to visit his house and give an appraisal. The dealer came and sniffed around the old man's treasures. Then, in a condescending manner, he said, "I'll give you five pounds (eight dollars) for the lot." The face of the old man fell. He had not expected much, but he had thought his collection was more valuable than that. Then the dealer turned and pointed to something hanging on a nail in the wall. It was just a piece of bronze attached to a colored ribbon. "But I'll give you a hundred pounds for that," he said. The old man's demeanor changed. He stood erect and went over to the piece of bronze, which was fashioned in the shape of a cross. He fondled it proudly. Things might be tough but they were not as bad as that. What he held in his hands was the Victoria Cross, the highest honor for gallantry that his grateful country could bestow. "I'll not part with that," he said. "My king pinned that medal on my chest." Only a piece of bronze! But it was a precious symbol more important to that man than food or drink.

Symbols help us to express the inexpressible. This is why the Christian faith—and especially the Christmas story—is so rich in them. The stable, the manger, the innocent young mother, the helpless infant Jesus—all send out powerful visual messages which help us grasp a little of the meaning of two of the most colossal words which, as we have already seen, lie at the heart of our faith.

The first of these words is *immanence*—the conviction that God is not "out there" but here, among us, down where we live. At heart we are all like the child who asked his parents where God was. When his father replied, "God is everywhere," the child said, "But I want God to be *somewhere*." In response to this longing to see God, Christmas calls out, "Hurry to Bethlehem. When you look at the baby in the manger, you are looking at God." The cradle is the symbol of God's immanence. Emmanuel means "God with us."

The second of these two words is *transcendence*. God is hid in light and is beyond the grasp of human reason. We cannot fathom the mystery of the Holy One, the Creator. The star which is far beyond us is a symbol of this "otherness" of God.

On the fourth Sunday of Advent we travel to Bethlehem, where we find these two tremendous concepts, symbolized by the cradle and the star, brought together as a baby rests in the arms of young, humble, obedient Mary. Here the symbols help us to understand the thrilling eternal truths which are bound up in these two great words of faith.

The call of Bethlehem—to wonder at God's love expressed in human form.

When I was about twelve years old, I was taken to my first philharmonic concert. It was produced specially for school-children. "You are in for a treat," our music teacher said enthusiastically. "You will hear a great orchestra and one of the finest choirs in the country." The bus taking us to the city where the concert was to be held was delayed. We arrived at the last minute and, breathless with anticipation, I took my seat in the balcony. I absorbed the scene in wonder. The vast choir was already in place. On the platform were men and women playing instruments the like of which I had never seen before, but this was not my idea of music, and soon my glee had changed to terrible disappointment. What a letdown! At that moment I did not realize that what I thought was the first number was in fact merely the orchestra tuning up!

And then an expectant hush descended upon the packed hall. The choir rose and this was the signal for the audience to erupt into applause as the distinguished conductor, immaculate in his formal suit, a white carnation in his buttonhole, made his entrance. He took his place on the rostrum, tapped with his baton, and pointed to the timpani. They rolled and suddenly orchestra and choir filled the air with the majestic music of the national anthem. It was spine-tinglingly thrilling. I had never heard anything like it before, and for the rest of the program I was spellbound. From that moment on music became a vital part of my life.

In the fields outside Bethlehem an angel delivered the announcement of the Savior's birth. The concluding words of the message were like a baton brought down to signal all the host of heaven to burst into song. And what were these words? *"This shall be a sign unto you; ye shall find the babe wrapped in swaddling clothes, lying in a manger."* That was it! Luke then goes on to say, *"And suddenly there was with the angel a multitude of the heavenly host praising God"* (Luke 2:12-13 KJV).

It would have been a momentous thing had God come to rule robed in glory and majesty. But heaven bursts into rapture because God did something even more wonderful. The Holy One came as a baby, slept in a manger, and lay in the warmest of cradles, the arms of a loving mother. God Almighty reached out tiny fingers to touch, whimpered when hungry, and became utterly dependent upon a young woman's care. Here we have displayed the immanence of God, who became vulnerable and one with us. Some years later in one of the greatest Christian works ever penned, John the apostle would describe this event in imperishable words: "And the Word became flesh and lived among us, and we have seen his glory, the glory as of a father's only son, full of grace and truth" (John 1:14).

Our joy in the Savior's birth is tempered, however, by a sense of awe and even of sorrow. Another symbol rises in our minds alongside those of cradle and star. It is the symbol of a cross upon a hill. The sublime event of this baby's birth is part of God's great redemptive plan, which is destined to include pain and desolation. Before God's purpose is accomplished, Mary will have earned the name later ages would give her, "Mother of Sorrows." Christian art offers us two pictures of her holding her son. In the first she is cradling Jesus as a baby and we can almost hear her singing a lullaby. In the second, the *Pietà*, she has across her lap his lifeless form after the crucifixion. The road from Bethlehem will lead to Calvary where, as Paul expresses it, "in Christ God was reconciling the world to himself."

In one of the Sunday school rooms of the church in which I was brought up, there was a print of one of Holman Hunt's most famous paintings, *The Shadow of Death*. It depicts Jesus as a young man who has completed his work at the carpenter's bench for the day. He is standing, stretching his limbs for relief after being cramped up. His arms are outstretched, and the sun throws the shadow of his form on the wall behind him, and it looks like a cross. The artist is saying through his picture that the cross was there before Jesus began to preach in Galilee. Of course Holman Hunt was right, but the truth is that the cross was there much earlier. In an eighteenth-century Christmas hymn one stanza says:

> Like Mary, let us ponder in our mind
> God's wondrous love in saving lost mankind;
> Trace we the Babe, who has retrieved our loss,
> From the poor manger to the bitter cross.
> *(John Byrom, 1692–1763)*

Bethlehem calls us to wonder. Here is set before our eyes the amazing love of God's redemptive plan. Only by taking human form could God redeem a lost humanity. The cradle points to a divine love willing to take this incomprehensible step, lay aside all the glory of divinity, and become a baby. The transcendent God becoming wondrously immanent. God with us. No wonder the hosts of heaven sang!

The comfort of Bethlehem—to rejoice in everlasting hope.

Christmas is about two decrees and two books.

The first decree was issued from the court of Augustus, Emperor of Rome, the most powerful man alive. He decreed that the world should be enrolled for tax purposes, and his legions saw to it that his word was obeyed. The names of all Roman subjects were thus duly entered in Caesar's book.

The second decree was issued not from a human court but from the court of heaven. It declared that God planned for all people to be enrolled in another book—the Book of Life. Unlike Caesar's book, this would not be transient but eternal. On that first Christmas night, to those living at that time, it must have seemed that all might and power belonged to Augustus. History, however, has handed down a different verdict. It is ironic that the great Caesar Augustus is now remembered by most people only because of the part he played in the story of that baby nursed by a peasant girl in a stable. Caesar in Rome represents *the transient;* the baby resting in his mother's arms represents *the eternal*.

I love Christmas! With festive decorations throughout the house, I find it a joyful time. We are not embarrassed at our childlike delight in receiving seasonal greetings from friends far and near. Each one is cherished. We eagerly read the glad news these messages bring: a new baby, a wedding in the family, or perhaps, new grandchildren. Our Christmas joy is enhanced by sharing the gladness of our friends.

But other messages also arrive in the mail during this season. We open a Christmas envelope and find, with the card, a note that tells a different story. It happens every year. Indeed two such messages came this very morning. The first read: "You will be sorry to hear that two months ago Arthur died." The second in the same mail carried the words, "We have been stunned by the loss of our darling daughter just six weeks ago." Suddenly we find ourselves on a roller coaster of emotion. From laughter we are plunged into tears. The song of the angels is hushed and the lights of Christmas are dimmed as we glimpse into the dark abyss of death. Our frail hearts whisper "Is this the end?"

My mother-in-law died suddenly one Christmas. She was relatively young, and naturally we were overwhelmed with sorrow. Loving friends expressed concern that so dark a shadow had been cast upon such a happy season. We were greatly helped by what someone wrote who looked at this sad event from a different perspective. "Do not think of the shadow which this sorrow has cast over your Christmas," he said. "Think rather of the light which Christmas sheds upon this sorrow." Advent hope! God's eternal promise which first brought that hope to birth long ago, as we have seen in the tents of Abraham and Isaac and in the gleaning fields with Ruth, has reached its glorious fulfillment in the coming of Jesus.

The cradle and the star, symbols of God's immanence and transcendence, stand before us in our sorrow, our fear, and our pain. They beckon us to look to God, to discover in the transient events of Bethlehem an everlasting significance. Here God has stepped decisively into human affairs and in doing so has defeated death and all other terrors. We can, therefore, bring our tired and frightened spirits to the crib of the Christ Child and there find comfort. Then we discover not only Advent *hope* but also Advent *joy*.

The challenge of Bethlehem—to become part of God's grand design.

Huckleberry Finn tells us that when the Widow Douglas told him about Moses and the bulrushes he was in quite a sweat to find out all about him. But author Mark Twain goes on to relate that when Huckleberry Finn discovered that Moses had been dead for a long time he was able to dismiss the story from his mind. "I don't take no stock in dead people," he said. Since it was just history, he did not need to concern himself about it.

The delightful nativity pageants, in which characters appear in the costume of biblical times, give us a comforting sense of distance. We find it is so easy to be like Huckleberry Finn and think of the story of the birth of Jesus as just history. Then there is no need for us to get into a sweat about it. But to find such complacent peace of mind we must avoid thinking about Mary. She is disturbing, even frightening, and she stabs our spirits broad awake. Her willingness, in all her youthful innocence, to become part of God's grand design for the salvation of the world, even though it would involve shame, humiliation, and the unkind gossiping tongues of Nazareth, shatters our easygoing complacency. Mary becomes more than history. She becomes a symbol of the life of faith which, if it is to be real, must be embodied in commitment and obedience.

A preacher friend of mine used to tell of a man who, on his way to his office, passed a building site where the new headquarters of a large bank was being erected. As a hobby this man worked in stone, and therefore, he was particularly interested in a stonemason who was chiseling at a piece of marble. He paused to watch but the craftsman was too engrossed in his work to notice him. Each day as he passed, he would pause to see how the work progressed, and to admire the work of the stonemason. One morning, as he watched, the stonemason happened to look up and their eyes met. The onlooker smiled and complimented the craftsman on his work. The other nodded his thanks. "Where will this piece of marble fit when you have finished your work?" the onlooker asked. "I don't know," the mason replied. "I haven't seen the plans. I just trust the architect and do my part as best I can."

Mary did not know the whole of God's wondrous redemptive plan. What she did know was that there was a part in it for her, and in faithful obedience she was ready to play that part to the full. She demonstrated her faith not through fine-sounding words but in placing her whole self at the disposal of God. She shines out in a world of compromise as a symbol of complete commitment to the divine will.

No passage of scripture is more powerful than Mary's song (Luke 1:46-55). She reaches back into the history of her people and links the promises given to past ages with what was about to happen in her life. "[God] has helped his servant Israel [Jacob], / in remembrance of his mercy, / according to the promise he made to our ancestors, / to Abraham and to his descendants forever" (Luke 1:54-55). But she does more than just look back across the centuries. With the eye of faith she looks into the future, beyond the birth of the

Savior to the end of history when God will end the injustices of the ages and establish a rule of righteousness.

Mary accepted the challenge to become part of God's grand design and allow her life to be used. She challenges us as we journey toward Bethlehem to follow her example and allow God to use us to bring nearer the fulfillment of the divine will. The test of our commitment to God's plan is to be seen not in our words but in our deeds. It is what we *are,* not merely what we *say,* which is the real test.

In his book *What Is a Christian* (Abingdon Press, 1962, p. 21), Leonard Griffith tells how one day the philosopher Josiah Royce was sitting in his study at Harvard University talking with a young student. In the course of the conversation the student asked the professor, "What is your definition of a Christian?" The great philosopher replied, "I do not know how to define a Christian. . . . But wait," he added, looking out the window, "there goes Phillips Brooks." What he was saying was that you cannot define Christianity in words; it must be embodied in a life, and this man so lived the life of faith that he had become part of God's plan to establish the reign of love and righteousness. He was an Advent person.

Early in his ministry, Phillips Brooks visited the Holy Land and chanced to be in Bethlehem on Christmas Day. As a result, in this season, Christians all over the world who know nothing of his historic ministry in Boston are blessed through the words he was moved to write while there:

> O little town of Bethlehem, how still we see thee lie;
> Above thy deep and dreamless sleep the silent stars go by.
> Yet in thy dark streets shineth the everlasting light;
> The hopes and fears of all the years are met in thee tonight.

Above all our hopes and fears we place the cradle and the star to remind us of God's immanence and transcendence. These two symbols come together at Bethlehem to call us to wonder, to comfort us with a glimpse of the eternal, and to challenge us to take part in carrying out God's design. Let our response to this wondrous event be to offer our lives in homage at the manger, and Christ will be reborn in us. If this happens, our celebration will become a time of spiritual renewal and our Advent journey will end with a Christmas experience which is gloriously different!

Study Questions

1. Read Luke 2:8-14, Luke 22:14-20, Mark 1:9-11, John 13:1-10. These passages all relate to symbols and symbolic acts. Make a list of the symbols which play a part both in your own life (such as the exchange of rings, a handshake, an embrace, an exchange of greeting cards, etc.) and also in the worship of the church (such as vestments the clergy may wear, the "furniture" of the church—pulpit, font, altar, etc.). Do such symbols help us to see the reality to which they point or do they become ends in themselves? How can we ensure that our use of symbols enriches our personal and devotional lives and do not become ends in themselves?

2. Read Matthew 2:1-12. What do you think was the significance of each of the three gifts the Wise Men brought to Bethlehem? In a poem set to music by Gustav Holst, which has become a much-loved carol, Christina Rossetti (1830–1894) includes the verse:

> What can I give him, poor as I am?
> If I were a shepherd, I would bring a lamb;
> If I were a Wise Man, I would do my part;
> Yet what I can I give him: give my heart.

What do you mean when you say "I give my heart"? What are the treasures *you* can bring to the Christ Child?

3. Compare the stories of Mary the mother of Jesus in Luke 1:26-56 and Hannah the mother of Samuel in 1 Samuel 1:1-2, 10. In particular, compare the songs of Hannah (1 Sam. 2:1-10) and Mary (Luke 1:46-55). What do you consider to be the themes these songs have in common? Do they have a message for us as we prepare to celebrate Christmas? What would you say this message is?

4. Read the hymn "O Little Town of Bethlehem." The author, Phillips Brooks, refers to "the hopes and fears of all the years."

What do you think were the hopes and fears which met in Bethlehem so long ago? What are the hopes and fears of our day that occupy your mind this Christmas? What light does the coming of Christ shed upon them?

5. During this week read the first chapter of each of the four Gospels. What do you consider to be the most striking differences among them? What light does each of them shed on the picture we have of Jesus?

Focus for the Week

As we approach Bethlehem we celebrate the transcendence and the immanence of God. It is all a miracle of grace. Bethlehem reminds us that in God's saving plan even the most lowly have a place. Paul celebrated this great truth when he wrote: "God chose what is foolish in the world to shame the wise; God chose what is weak in the world to shame the strong; God chose what is low and despised in the world, things that are not, to reduce to nothing things that are" (1 Cor. 1:27-28). As we respond to the call of Bethlehem, we bow in wonder. As we respond to the comfort of Bethlehem, our hearts are made strong by resting in the promise of eternal life in Christ. As we respond to the challenge of Bethlehem, we come to offer our lives in the service of Christ. Led from the cradle to the star, this Christmas can be a time of spiritual renewal.